How to Use Your Extra Belly Button Lint

JOSHUA KAIN

CONTENT

DISCLAIMER

This is a work of creative nonfiction. Some parts, particularly the guidelines, uses, procedures, and jokes have been fictionalized in various degrees for creative and entertainment purposes. While every effort has been made to ensure the fun facts presented in this book are accurate, the guidelines, uses, procedures, and jokes are light-hearted and cursory, and should not replace professional advice. The guidelines, uses and procedures that follow should not be attempted without further research and without taking on board the specialist knowledge of genuine experts in these fields. The author and publisher do not assume and hereby disclaim any liability to any party for any loss, damage, or disruption caused by errors or omissions, whether such errors or omissions result from negligence, accident, or any other cause. This book is for entertainment purposes only. Readers should seek professional advice as appropriate.

INTRODUCTION

Welcome to the weird and wonderful world of belly button lint! If you've ever found yourself exploring the uncharted territories that lie beneath your shirt, pondering life's greatest mysteries—like why socks always disappear in the laundry or whether cats are secretly plotting world domination—then this book is for you. "How to Use Your Extra Belly Button Lint" is here to celebrate the absurd, the quirky, and the downright silly aspects of our existence.

Now, you might be wondering, why on earth would anyone want to write a book about belly button lint? Well, dear reader, why not? In a world filled with serious pursuits and never-ending responsibilities, sometimes we need to take a step back, have a good laugh, and embrace the hilarity that life throws our way. Belly button lint may be small, but it's a reminder that joy can be found in the most unexpected places.

In the next chapter, we're diving headfirst into general guidelines to help you understand the linty depths of your belly button. Prepare to be amazed, amused, and possibly a little perplexed as we explore the sacred belly fluff together. Remember to loosen that belt and let your belly breathe. It's time to appreciate the lint that gathers in the mysterious crater also known as navel fluff. So, grab your tweezers, put on your imagination cap, and let the lintertainment begin!

COLLECTION TECHNIQUES

Ah, the art of belly button lint collection —for many, a hobby turned profession. This procedure requires precision, dedication, and perhaps the occasional sniff. The following steps may seem simple, but they are necessary to equip yourself with the knowledge needed.

Types of Navel Fluff

There are three types of lint one might come across: the soft, waxy, and rigid. Soft fluff has a cloud-like texture, delicate to the touch much like soft cotton candy. Waxy fluff's texture is akin to a blend of beeswax and stringy lint, making it unique and one of the rarest among the belly button lint family. Finally, the rigid fluff almost always comes out together in one clump due to its longer fermentation periods.

Mental Preparation

Delicately extracting belly button lint is a skill that is difficult to master and leaves many disappointed, knowing they've left some fluff behind.

It is important to ensure you are in a focused state of mind to allow for proper extraction. Remember, patience is a virtue, so approach each pluck with a steady hand and no distractions during the process.

Tools of the Trade

The most important step of any operation is meticulous preparation. Your kit must be ready by your side, finely selected for the specific characteristic of lint you're about to extract. Each type of lint requires a different set of tools.

> ***Soft fluff***: Tweezers or any resemblance of tiny tongs
> ***Waxy fluff***: Any scoop of your choice (must be small enough to fit your belly button)
> ***Rigid fluff***: Your good ol' fingers

Storage of the Navel Fluff

Once you've delicately plucked your collection of belly button lint, the crucial question arises: where does one store these precious treasures?

The good news is that any container of your choice will do. The key is to keep your collection in a place that brings you joy. As you admire your collection, you might be wondering, "What on Earth can I do with all this navel fluff?" Fear not! In the following chapter, we'll explore 43 creative uses for your belly button fluff that go beyond mere storage.

43 BELLY BUTTON LINT USES

Abstract Art

Create unique abstract art by having belly button lint as the main medium. The best thing is that the possibilities are endless! You can arrange the lint into interesting patterns or random shapes on a canvas or even mix with resin to create a mosaic.

Turn it Into Yarn

Start by collecting a sufficient amount of lint, and gently tease apart the fibers, fluffing them up to create a soft and pliable texture. For added strength and cohesion, mix the lint with a small amount of hair conditioner or fabric softener. Begin spinning the fibers between your fingers, gradually forming a makeshift yarn. Continue this process until you achieve the desired thickness and consistency.

Gift as a Conversation Starter

Choose a jar of any size to store your lint collection; however, make sure that the interior is clean and dry. Consider adding small decorative elements, such as colorful ribbons or a label that says "Belly Button Lint Collection – Handle with Care!"

Stress Ball

Find a small balloon and carefully stretch the opening to make it easier to fill. Use a funnel or make one with a piece of paper to funnel the lint into the balloon. Fill the balloon with the lint until you achieve your desired level of firmness. Tie a knot at the end of the balloon to secure the lint inside.

Sell Your Lint Online

Selling your belly button lint online is a fun way to connect with fellow belly button lint enthusiasts. Choose a suitable online platform for selling quirky items, such as a niche marketplace or an auction site.

Emergency Fire Starter

Begin by collecting a small amount of dry and clean lint from your belly button. Place the lint at the center of your fire pit or kindling. Use additional dry twigs, leaves, or other combustible materials to build upon the flame.

Crafty Christmas Ornaments

Remove the top of the clear ornament and use a funnel to fill it with the lint, creating layers or patterns for visual interest. Consider adding a few small decorative elements of your choice like tiny jingle bells or colorful ribbons inside the ornament. Once filled, securely place the ornament top back on.

Custom-made Teddy Bear

Find or purchase a plain teddy bear or plush toy as your base. You can even make your own if you have the skills and material! Stuff the teddy bear with the collected belly button lint, and sew the teddy bear back up.

Hourglass

Find two identical clear plastic bottles with secure lids. Remove the labels and clean the bottles thoroughly. Once dry, carefully funnel the lint into one of the bottles, allowing it to settle evenly. Attach the second bottle securely to the first, forming an hourglass shape. Seal the connection with strong adhesive to prevent any lint from escaping. Turn the hourglass over, and watch the lint move from one bottle to the other.

Tiny Pillow Stuffing

Craft small, pillow-sized fabric squares or choose pre-made miniature pillowcases for convenience. Stuff the pillowcases with the belly button lint, then use a needle and thread or fabric glue to secure the edges, ensuring the lint stays neatly inside.

Lint-filled Snow Globe

Find a small, clear, waterproof container with a secure lid, such as a Mason jar or a plastic snow globe. Place the lint at the bottom of the container, creating a snowy base. Add miniature figurines like tiny snowmen or trees, securing them in place with waterproof glue. Fill the container with water, leaving a little space at the top to avoid overflow when sealing. Add a pinch of glitter for extra sparkle. Carefully seal the lid, ensuring it's airtight to prevent leakage.

Miniature sculptures

Shape a small amount of belly button lint into the basic form of your sculpture. It could be an animal, character, or any shape you have in mind. Use a felting needle to poke and compact the lint fibers. The barbs on the needle will help bind the fibers together, gradually creating a more solid structure. Be patient and work slowly to achieve the desired shape.

Confetti Cannon

Collect the belly button lint, a paper towel roll, and a balloon. Seal one end of the paper towel roll and fill it with belly button lint. This end will be the bottom of your confetti cannon. Stretch a balloon over the open end of the roll, securing it with tape. Pull down on the balloon, and release to enjoy a burst of lint confetti!

Lint-Based Fertilizer

Give your plants a lint-based boost by mixing belly button lint into your garden soil for added nutrients.

Jewelry

You can use any piece of jewelry, such as earrings, bracelets, or necklaces. For this case, you can fill a pendant or locket with lint. You can wear the jewelry or gift it to someone!

Lint-filled Terrarium

Place belly button lint at the bottom of a large glass container. Add additional components of the terrarium, such as plants, moss, and rocks to complete the ecosystem.

Paper-mâché

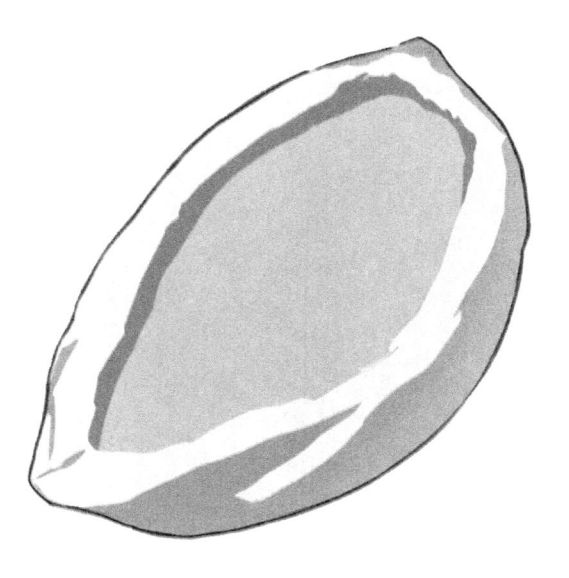

Mix white glue with water to create a paste and apply it to a base formed with belly button lint. Layer strips of newspaper over the molded belly button lint, allowing each layer to dry before adding the next. Shape the project as desired and let it thoroughly dry. Once dry, paint and decorate the exterior of your design.

Lint Beard

Using non-toxic glue or adhesive, attach the pieces of lint to your face in the desired beard shape.

Linty Clay

Mix the dry belly button lint with a standard clay recipe, combining it thoroughly until the lint is evenly distributed.

Linty Paper

Create a paper pulp by blending the lint with water until it forms a thick, textured consistency. Spread the mixture evenly on a flat surface, pressing out excess water, and let it air dry. The result is a lint-based paper, perfect for any creative paper project.

Lint keychain pompoms

Shape the lint into small pompoms, either by rolling it into compact balls or by using a small sphere as a base. Attach a small loop of colorful string or a keyring to the lint pompom to create a keychain.

Scrapbook

Document the various lint creations over the years by making your own belly button lint scrapbook.

Linty Aromatherapy

Place lint sachets around your home, claiming each color emits a different fragrance, even if they all just smell like, well, belly button lint.

Linty Advent Calendar

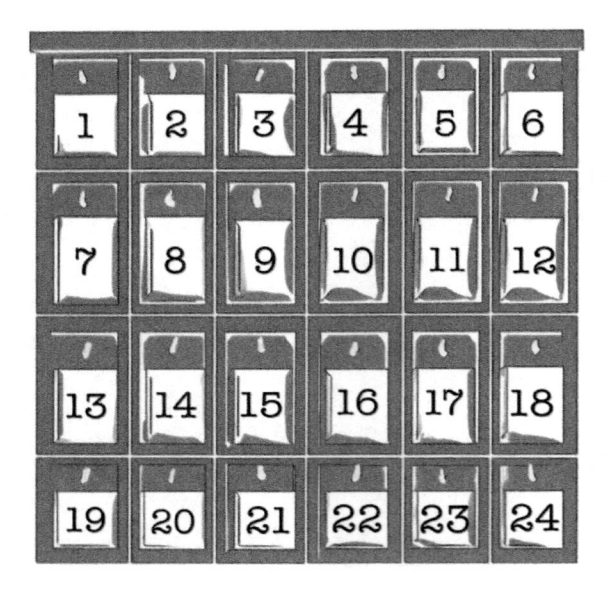

Add a touch of humor and surprise to the holiday season by incorporating belly button lint into your homemade advent calendar.

Scented candles

Mix the scented lint with the melted wax when preparing your candles, allowing the fragrance to disperse as the candle burns. Pour the wax into your chosen candle molds, ensuring the lint is evenly distributed.

Soap

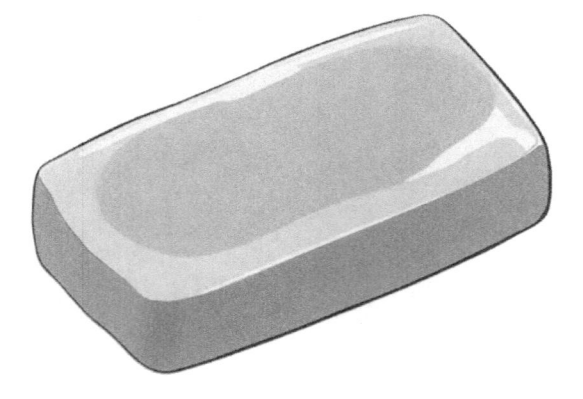

Mix the lint with your soap base during the melting process and pour the mixture into molds to create unique and textured soap bars.

Nail Art

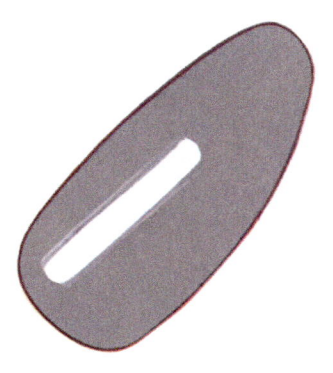

Belly button lint can be used in several ways in nail art. One of the methods includes adding sprinkled lint to the topcoat for a textured design.

Dreamcatcher

Use the belly button lint yarn to weave it into a
dreamcatcher design.

Play with it

This one is pretty self-explanatory!

Lint-cushioned hangers

Glue pieces of belly button lint to the edges of the hanger's frame to allow for a non-slip surface when hanging clothes.

Packing material

Use lint as padding or cushioning when packing fragile items for shipping or storage.

Emergency Insulation

In cold weather, stuff gaps in windows or doors with belly button lint for temporary insulation.

Absorbent Media

Use belly button lint to soak up spills. Its fibrous nature can effectively absorb and trap moisture.

Plant Insulation

Surround the base of your potted plants with a layer of lint to help regulate soil temperature, retain moisture, and protect the roots from extreme temperatures. The lint acts as a soft barrier, providing a cozy environment for your plants to thrive.

Time capsule

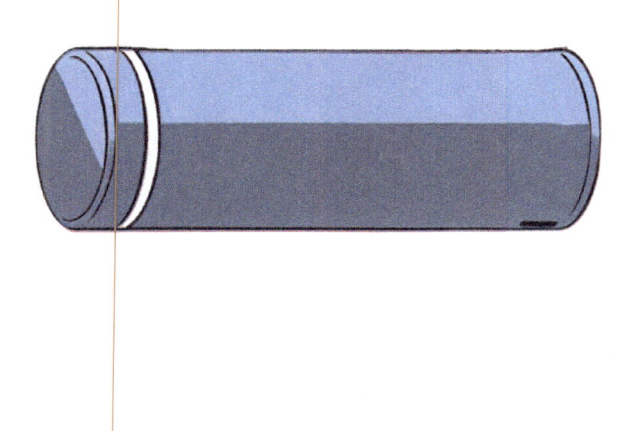

Create a belly button lint time capsule by preserving lint from different periods of your life.

Fishing Bait

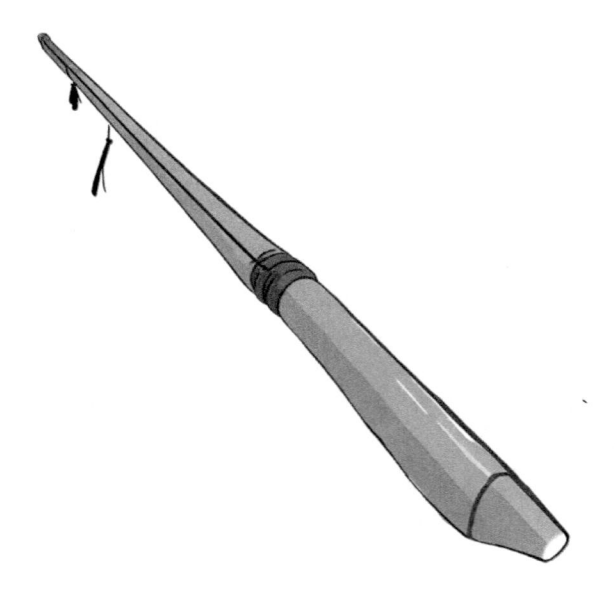

Fish are often attracted to scents, and the natural fibers of lint can absorb and hold onto various scents effectively. Roll the scented lint into small balls or use it to cover traditional bait like worms.

Bird Nest

Leave lint out for the birds to use in building their nests.

Dust collector

Use your belly button lint to clean delicate surfaces like keyboards, antique vases, or your pet's ears. Just be careful not to leave any stray lint-balls behind.

Door mat

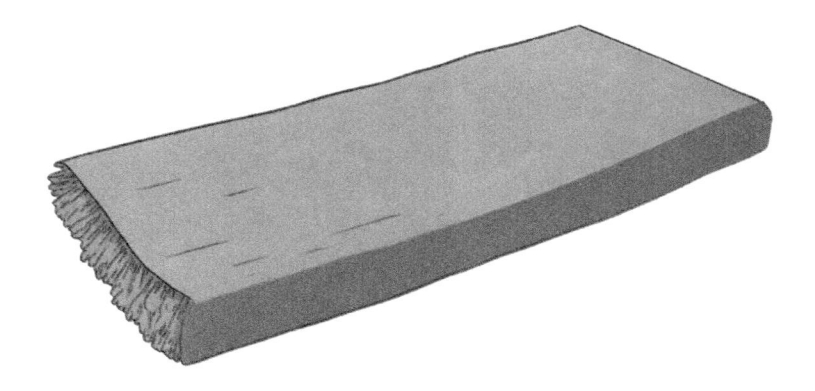

Attach the lint to a plain or pre-made door mat using a strong adhesive or by sewing it directly onto the surface.

Make a fragrance

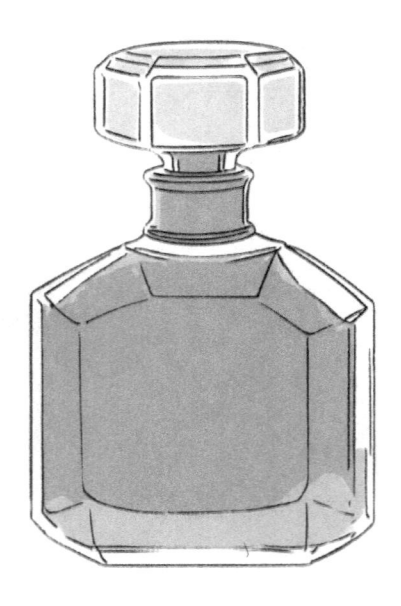

Infuse your own belly button lint with your favorite scents. Add a few drops of your preferred essential oils or fragrance oils, allowing the lint to absorb the scent. Seal the container and let it sit for a day or two, allowing the fragrance to permeate the lint.

Lint Pin Cushion

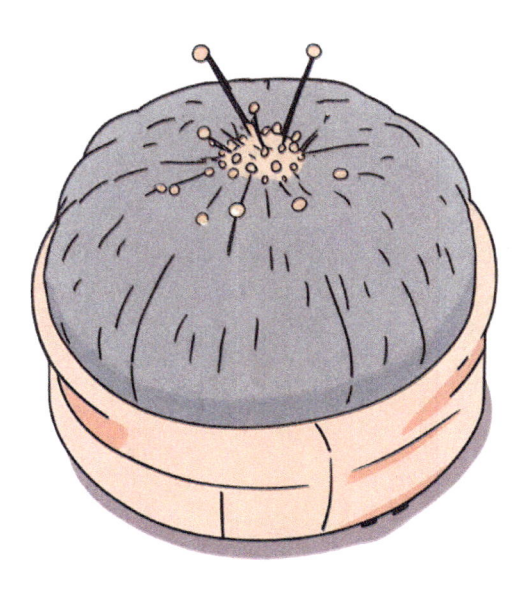

Stuff a small fabric pouch or a pre-made pin cushion with the lint, creating a soft and pliable surface for your pins and needles.

Pot Scrubber

Collect clean and dry lint, and tightly pack it into a small, breathable pouch or mesh bag. Tie or sew the bag securely, creating a lint-filled scrubber that can be used to tackle light cleaning tasks in your kitchen.

Tickle someone with it

Do with this information as you wish.

52

FUN FACTS

1. A scientist, Karl Kruszelnicki, from the University of Sydney won an Ig Nobel Prize in 2002, a satiric prize awarded for achievements in science that first make people laugh then make them think, for conducting the world's first belly button lint survey.

2. Older hairy males with a belly button pointed inwards are more likely to have belly button lint.

3. Belly button lint is scientifically named "navel fluff" but referred to more frequently as the acronym "BBL", which stands for Belly Button Lint, in scientific literature.

4. Shaving the hair around your belly reduces your chances of having belly button lint.

5. Belly button lint is composed of a mixture of clothing fibers, skin cells, and body hair.

6. There are almost 70 different kinds of bacteria sitting in the average belly button.

7. There is a Guinness World Record Holder for having the largest collection of belly button lint. The Australian librarian, Graham Barker, has collected 22.1 grams of belly button lint in jars for 26 years. Talk about dedication!

8. The term "belly button" comes from the Old English word "belg," meaning bag or pouch.

9.   The artist, Rachel Betty Case, from Bethlehem, Pennsylvania, collects belly button lint from her male friends to create miniature bears. She stores them in jars, and sells her artwork online!

10. There is a project known as the Belly Button Fluff Project, which aims to recycle belly button fluff into clothing as a step towards reducing the environmental footprint of the textile industry. They conducted research and claim that belly button fluff is a material softer than cotton, wool, and silk combined!

11. The belly button is a leftover part of the umbilical cord, which is an organ that shared blood between the mother and baby during pregnancy.

12. The shape of your belly button doesn't depend on how the doctor cuts the umbilical cord during birth.

13. Wearing older shirts reduces the amount of belly button lint formed.

14. People with a snail trail are more likely to have belly button lint.

15. The color of belly button lint varies with peoples' skin tone. People with lighter skin tones have lighter belly button lint, whereas people with darker skin tones have darker belly button lint.

16. The color of lint can also be affected depending on the color of the clothing worn over the belly button.

17. There is an experiment known as the Hair-free Highway experiments, where participants shaved the hair around their belly button to see if there is any effect on lint.

18. Only 10% of the world population have a belly button pointing outwards!

19. It is quite normal for a belly button to have a mild odor. Although, a very smelly belly button is not usually a good sign.

20. Omphalophobia is the fear of belly buttons! This type of phobia involves avoiding or being terrified of the belly button. People with this fear can have anxiety, panic attacks, and avoid situations where the belly buttons are visible.

21. The medical term for the belly button is "umbilicus."

22. The average person produces around 1 gram of belly button lint a year.

23. Navel-gazing, also known as omphaloskepsis, is the act of looking at or thinking about your belly button to help you relax and meditate.

24. The belly button is celebrated in some parts of the world. There is a festival held each year in Shibukawa, Japan, where people paint their bellies and dance with their belly buttons out. Shibukawa city is considered the belly button of Japan, specifically at the belly button rock in Shinmachi Gosaro.

25. The historical belly button rock in Shinmachi Gosaro is also known as belly button jizo. It is believed that if you pray while caressing it, your wishes might come true. Some even say it can help make wishes for pregnancy come true.

26. Some people are born without a belly button! Although, it is a very rare occurrence.

27. Poking your belly button can touch deep fibers that send signals to your spinal cord. Sometimes, your spinal cord might get the message wrong, making you feel like you need to pee.

28. The texture of belly button lint can be affected by factors like humidity and the type of laundry detergent used.

29. Belly button lint production tends to decrease with age.

30. Ancient Egyptians considered the belly button to be the center of a person's being.

31. The accumulation of belly button lint tends to be higher in for men than in women.

32. Up until the 1980s, it was illegal for women to show their belly buttons in public in America.

33. Humans aren't the only ones with belly buttons. In fact, most mammals, including dogs, have belly buttons!

34. The body's energy wheels, or chakras, run from the head to the base of the spine, including the solar plexus or "navel chakra." This energy center, much like the belly button, is crucial for a smooth flow of energy. When blocked, it may leave you feeling powerless or irritable. The concept originates from ancient Indian traditions, particularly within yoga and Ayurveda.

JOKES

1. Why did the belly button lint apply for a job? It wanted to get into the naval industry.

2. Why did the belly button want to get famous? It wanted to be the center of attention.

3. Why did the belly button lint go to therapy? It had too many issues coming to the surface.

4. How does belly button lint keep in touch? Through the naval mail service.

5. How does a belly button say goodbye? "Belly nice knowing you!"

6. Why did the belly button lint refuse to leave the party? It was stuck in the naval.

7. Why was the belly button always chosen as team captain? It had the best center!

8. How did the belly button lint become a detective? It had a talent for navalgazing.

9. Why did the belly button lint start a YouTube channel? It wanted to go viral.

10. Why did the belly button lint get a promotion at work? It rose to the surface.

11.   What's the belly button's favorite band? Lintin' Park.

12.   Why did the belly button lint attend therapy? It had separation anxiety.

13.   How does a belly button express excitement? It does the belly dance!

14.   Why did the belly button break up with the lint? It found someone less clingy!

15.   What did the belly button lint say when it was late for the meeting? "Sorry, I got caught up in a tight spot!"

16.   How does a belly button make decisions? It goes with its gut feeling!

Printed in Great Britain
by Amazon

54886938R00046